The Early James Joyce

by

NATHAN HALPER

 **Columbia University Press**

NEW YORK & LONDON 1973

COLUMBIA ESSAYS ON MODERN WRITERS
is a series of critical studies of English,
Continental, and other writers whose works are of contemporary
artistic and intellectual significance.

Editor

George Stade

Advisory Editors

Jacques Barzun   W.T.H. Jackson   Joseph A. Mazzeo

The Early James Joyce is Number 68 of the series

NATHAN HALPER
is the author of a number of critical
studies on James Joyce.

Library of Congress Cataloging in Publication Data

Halper, Nathan.
  The early James Joyce.

  (Columbia essays on modern writers, no. 68)
  Bibliography: p. 47–48
  1. Joyce, James, 1882–1941.   I. Title.
II. Series.
PR6019.09Z573   823′.9′12   72-13949
ISBN 0-231-03316-8

The Early James Joyce

It is wrong to think of Joyce as Stephen Dedalus. The Joyce who matters is the one who is himself. Stephen is a usual type of unusual young man.

There may be a few in any university. They feel that they have powers which are not being put to use: they are in a society which, to the loss of both, is not yet able to recognize the riches they could bring to it. In their impatience, they tend—even more —to find solace in themselves.

They are often frail; they may have trouble with their eyes. *← Bullshit* In the schoolboy world, they rank below their sturdier companions. They are often poor. There is frequently an added wound: they began in ease. (A pretension to gentility lays an extra chip upon their shoulder.)

Intelligence, skill with words, familiarity with books, gain a certain respect, but reveal that the boy is alien to the group. (An appraisal which he is willing to accept.)

Such a boy, eager to be like grown-ups, takes their attitudes and values. Older, he rejects them with even greater vehemence. He turns to a belief that is less limited and limiting, a goal that is more relevant to his picture of himself.

So far this is Stephen. It is less than Joyce. The biographies are similar. Joyce is capable of having Stephen's thoughts and feelings. But he is watching, he is considering, weighing and measuring his deeds and what he thinks and feels. Stephen is not unaware. Yet, no matter how far he goes in looking at himself, Joyce goes one step further: he exists in an additional dimension. This not only helps him write his books. It makes these books the particular books they are.

James Joyce was born in Dublin in 1882. Attracted to the Church, its logic, ritual, and symbols, he thought of being a priest, custodian of its tradition, agent of its mysteries. But when he looked around him, instead of an enlargement, he found petty-mindedness. Religion was a matter of phrases to be learned by rote. The gift that was wanted was his unquestioning docility.

In the secular field, there was a stirring of revolt. Again, uniformity was called for. The rebels had slogans. He was expected to repeat them. There were manifestoes. He was supposed to sign them. He, too, wanted to throw off the bridle of the master: yet he could not feel their piety, the prim adulation of Ireland as Kathleen.

Art alone could give him a sense of dignity and stature. Art would allow him to live—to express and realize himself.

But, if this young man was going to be a writer, the decision, by itself, did not mean that he would be a good one. Bright, touchy, self-centered—there are too many who fit this description. There are too many directions any one of them may take. Such a young man is the subject of *A Portrait.* There is little reason to foresee that Stephen could become its author.

Joyce's first publications were vigorous and solemn. In 1900, an essay, "Ibsen's New Drama," was taken by the *Fortnightly Review.* One year later, he wrote *The Day of the Rabblement;* then, in 1902, an essay on James Clarence Mangan. If these were not his, they would not merit our attention. Knowing that they are, we are able to recognize a phrase or sentiment that is related to something he said later. Even so, they are in a different voice. Too stiff, overpositive, the tones are those of one who has not, as yet, learned how to look at things in several ways at a time.

The author of the later books is at the opposite extreme. The distance is so great that Joyce's being able to traverse it is not totally explained by saying he matured or by dwelling on some crisis that, as one of its effects, brought a wider vision. There is something more. The writer of the essays, even if they do not show it, has already traveled part of his journey to *Finnegans Wake*.

There is a tendency to think of Joyce as changing, like a tadpole, in the interval between his books. Though we understand one, we have to start afresh to understand a second. And, with each new book, this becomes more difficult. It is better if we see that the writer of the *Wake* (in a more inhibited form) is present in the first one. It makes each of them clearer.

In college, Joyce was a reader of Bruno and Nicholas of Cusa. He knew of a Unity which is also Diversity. In a universe of varying and contradictory phenomena, there is a principle which informs them with coherence. Yet the principle reveals itself only in the infinite and ever-changing phenomena.

Such a universe refused to fit into the simplicities of language: there was always something that spilled over. He was used to unequivocal answers. He no longer could accept them: yet he was still in the tradition where one attempted to give them. Able to renounce the dogma in which he had been taught, he had not lost the habit of casting even his doubt into a dogmatic form. He showed intolerance to those who did not share the opinion he reached only yesterday and might qualify tomorrow.

His work would be rooted in the life he knew, that of lower middle-class Dublin. But, in dealing with its values, he must not allow himself to share them. He had to have an area of uninvolvement, room in which he could observe, order, consider, and

[5]

transmute. To keep this distance, he must be able to resist the temptation to be soft to what was, after all, his own and in many ways dear.

The puritanical zeal, the rigor he discarded in his personal life he translated to his work. He must not charm: he must not let himself be charmed by any of the in-groups of the literary community. For the greater glory of his god, he became an inquisitor, harsh with others as well as with himself.

There was a new, yet already-traditional polarity: the Artist and his Society. Joyce felt that he must show the position he had taken. A battle is no place in which to lean over backwards. Here an overstatement is a more accurate expression than a fair, balanced, and even-handed remark. As a crusader, he was warrior and priest. And in neither capacity could he give the enemy his due.

There was also place for less high-minded activity. Joy in battle per se: Dublin joy in polishing the barb and dipping it in Dublin malice. Joy in contradicting. With it, relish in badgering the bourgeoisie. ("No man," he said in a paraphrase of Bruno, "can be a lover of the true or the good unless he abhors the multitude.") Mindful of his higher Purpose, he said only what he meant, but made a point of saying it in a way that startled and outraged.

It was partly a performance. Add the joy of the performer: joy in good lines: in a good part. (He may be the villain they dislike, but he feels that he is noticed.) When he bowed to Ibsen or in *The Day of the Rabblement* implied that he himself might be the other's successor, this met the specifications. Yet the words he used necessarily concealed his mischief and exuberance. The pose and its gestures, in spite of the motivation, depended for effect on his wearing an air of self-possession and solemnity.

In his essays, Joyce refused to be tentative, presenting his propositions not as something to be proved but as something proven. He shunned timid phrases like "it may be" or "I think," avoided "however" and "although." To him a Day of Judgment was primarily a Day of Wrath. Here are the saved. (They are few in number.) Here are the damned—no middle ground between them.

His role, that of the young man capable of writing such essays, helped his self-aggrandizement. But, for all of that, it involved a shrinking, a simplification of Joyce. He was more copious, less monochromatic. And, to that degree, this is a departure from himself.

Young people have energies they do not know how to direct. Like them, he watched, tried to fathom his world. Even more than most, he was self-watchful: tried to understand himself. But, with all his skills, he did not—in youth, could not—have the ones that were needed to encompass the totality, the currents and countercurrents, which he could sense in the world and in himself.

If he found a pose, that is not unusual. But where, as a rule, people tend to grow into their mask, he sought to reverse the process. He tried to get back to his face.

His early essays, then, have an interest beyond that of their small intrinsic merit. They are the first term in a series. After this, in the progression of his work, there were two opposing movements. Books became more elaborate, techniques increasingly complex. But, at each step, *Dubliners, A Portrait of the Artist, Ulysses, Finnegans Wake,* he dismantled more of the disguise. In the essays, it is easy to see a poor likeness. In the later work, seeing anything becomes more difficult. However, the image—if we make it out—is more and more like himself.

He would set up his flattering arrangement. But, for counterbalance, there was a second form of vanity which would not let him pitch the picture too far from himself. "This wart, that tic—these are also me." This humiliating episode, that undignified moment, the shame or pain—what others might not confess—would be gathered into a new likeness; but the pattern was arranged so that, with all its blemishes, it finally was self-enhancing.

He might think of himself as different from others. Yet, no matter where he looked, he would see an echo, a reminder: in every frame of reference, something related to himself. Conversely, looking at himself, he began to learn about the others. In returning to himself—each book a station—he also came back to the multitude which he had formerly abhorred.

As he grew older, he saw himself as a double of his father. He saw his son in his memories of youth. The future and the past were drawn into a continuum. He was the measure of this universe: even while the universe became the mirror of himself.

The aspects of the subject were increasingly painted by the different aspects of the painter. He put them against different backgrounds: he would look at them from different angles, in a varying light. All space in a nutshell, a nutshell in all space. He had always seen it. He began to show it. His emotions, his moods find their way into the picture. Agitation, nerve-ends—plus a greater objectivity. Irritation, grudges—and a growing charity. When Bloom or H. C. Earwicker feels the exacerbations of the moment, he does so in a framework of Eternity. The accumulations of fear, of guilt come in a texture of comedy.

That was later. The writer of the essays was not using his own voice. In the poems, with the aid of hindsight, we can see it starting to emerge. The earliest that has survived is, apparently, the villanelle that is quoted in *A Portrait.* With "langorous look and lavish limb"—

> Are you not weary of ardent ways,
> Lure of the fallen seraphim?

it resembles the poems (perhaps by Enoch Soames) that had been "modern" in England in the 1890s.

As Joyce got to know the song of the Elizabethans, especially of Dowland, his own became less regular. The length of different phrases and the pause between them formed a pattern that he played against the rhythms based on stress. The lyrics which in time were published in *Chamber Music* had occasional dissonance. They were laced with irony. (An occasional word had a second meaning, this not always seemly.) Even so, the irony was not enough. Like a dash of vinegar, in the tiny quantities used it only helped to bring out the sweetness. The unconventional touches were so unobtrusive that they blended into the old-fashioned ensemble.

The girls in these lyrics are like the poems themselves. They are bloodless, faceless—figurines congealed in the middle of a graceful moment. The bosom is mentioned, but this is merely an abstraction, a convention of the genre.

To Joyce, "man of letters" was subordinate to "poet." His songs were written by the former. They were minor variations on the minor themes of others. What he felt was filtered through the words of his originals—who had done it better.

As he was to realize, he was not a good poet. His strength always lay in the symphonic. His work requires a control, an ability to regulate the meshing and unmeshing of a universe of voices. It is at its best when the voices resist—barely are contained or barely manage to break through. In the lyrics, we can hear for a first time the whisper of a second voice. (This may be the reason why, when he wrote them, he regarded them so highly.) But, in the light of what he later did, the antiphonal voice is too faint. The verses are too slight.

Once a theme suggests itself, he runs it through it paces. He may have felt a poem deeply; but in the working out, it becomes an exercise, a schoolroom demonstration of how the thing should

[9]

be done. There is only one that has its own Necessity. "I Hear an Army" has echoes of the words of others, yet it not only begins with a compelling image, it keeps a turbulent momentum. Here—here only in the poems—we have two commensurate forces, the one trying to impose, the other to throw off the domination of the writer.

In a lecture which he gave in 1900, he quoted a character of Ibsen's. "I will let in fresh air." So, in "The Holy Office" (summer of 1904), he rejected the Dublin writers who "dream their dreamy dreams"—among them Yeats and Synge. As opposed to them, he presented himself. *He* was close to life. Honest, unafraid

> Firm as the mountain-ridges where
> I flash my antlers on the air.

It is hard to tell how much of the poem he meant. The truth: nothing but the truth. Truth at any cost. But it might be bent for the sake of a good line. The couplet lends itself to exaggeration. In such a poem, even a character admired—for example, the poet himself—is something of a comic figure.

In the interval between his lecture and the poem, he jotted down his "epiphanies." He wrote a play. (A few years later, he destroyed it.) An interview and reviews. An inferior version of "The Sisters." To justify his swanking, he might show "I Hear an Army," a single twelve-line lyric. And, despite its merits, this involved no opening of windows.

He had also begun *Stephen Hero,* an anticipation of *A Portrait of the Artist.* For the next few years, though with different results, he worked on this and the stories of *Dubliners.* In the latter, he was free to give new shape to the situation or incident that suggested a story. In *Stephen Hero,* by contrast, he had personal commitments. There were things he wanted to describe, comments he had to make about his environment, his

[10]

family, teachers, and friends, his writing, and himself. And, in doing so, he wanted to be sure that nobody would miss the point. The *i* is dotted. And if, understandably, the writer was dissatisfied with the pages that he saw unfolding, there was nonetheless something to which he could look forward, something to get upon the record. And—once again—he wanted nobody to miss the point.

Though they are related, the stories are separate units. He was able to weigh each in its turn: able to begin the next with the benefit of what he learned writing the one before it. In June, 1904, he met Nora Barnacle, with whom, in the autumn, he left for the Continent. In *Dubliners*, we see Joyce becoming conscious of his new condition, his new responsibilities. *Stephen Hero* has no sign of any change in the writer. He is propelled by the original impulse.

In 1907, he stopped work upon the novel. (He had been writing "The Dead"; one may surmise that the contrast was too great.) Using some of its material, he began *A Portrait of the Artist*.

There are those who prefer the early version. This usually means that they do not care for either. *Stephen Hero* may be a stick with which to beat *A Portrait*. As a thing in itself, a would-be work of art, it has little to commend it. One agrees with the author who left it. As biography, however—as *notes* for biography—the book has uses. For this purpose, its stodginess becomes a virtue. Among the items Joyce eventually pared, we occasionally find a detail that throws a light on his development as writer.

Walking through the streets, Stephen had "eyes and ears ever prompt to receive impressions." He made a "garner of words," reading Freeman or William Morris as one would "a thesaurus." In his verse, he tried to "fix the most elusive of his moods," putting the "lines together not word by word but syllable by syllable. He . . . . permuted and combined the five vowels to construct cries for primitive emotion."

This young man prefigures the writer of the later books. So, too, does a "taste for enigmatic roles" or an "importunate devil within him whose appetite was on edge for the farcical."

He who "persuaded himself that it is necessary for an artist to labor incessantly . . . if he wishes to express even the simplest conception" is a form of the Joyce who was to say he spent twelve hundred hours on the twenty pages of "Anna Livia" or spent a day in shifting six words of a sentence in *Ulysses* before he decided which order was nearest to doing what he wanted.

When Stephen finds that beauty consists "as much in the concealment as in the revelation of construction," he is speaking of the way that verses should be read: yet we are able to foresee how this statement will be extended by the writer to meaning as well as to construction—till it reaches and embraces the "hides and hints," the concealing and revealing that flower in *Finnegans Wake*.

It is harder to see Stephen as the author of *Stephen Hero*. Joyce gave Stephen tendencies that he noticed in himself. However, in this work, it is Joyce himself who fails to exhibit them. No "importunate devil," he is a Dr. Watson, who is awed by his subject.

"Stephen . . . strove to pierce to the significant heart of everything." The "supreme artist" is he "who could disentangle the subtle soul of the image from its mesh of defining circumstance . . . [then] re-embody it in artistic circumstances chosen as the most exact for it in its new office." Joyce does not put this into practice. He makes some improvements on what happened to himself, but there is little sign of his having tried to "re-embody" the material.

It is in this book that Joyce, through the lips of Stephen,

presents the concept of "epiphany." By epiphany he meant a "sudden spiritual manifestation." It is the moment when we recognize an object is "*that* thing which it is. Its soul, its whatness, leaps to us from the vestments of its appearance." It "was for the man of letters to record these . . . epiphanies with . . . care, seeing that they . . . are the most subtle and evanescent of moments."

Indeed, a notebook of epiphanies survives. If a reader fails to be impressed, he is not required to feel guilty. He is only doing what Joyce did later. Epiphanies are not mentioned in *A Portrait.* They are mentioned in *Ulysses*—only to be mocked by Stephen. It is even possible that Joyce already mocks them in *Stephen Hero* itself. Here a "trivial incident set him composing some ardent verses which he entitled a 'Villanelle of the Temptress.'" This is probably the villanelle ("Are you not weary of ancient ways?") which we noted in *A Portrait.*

Elsewhere we are told that when Stephen wrote his songs, it was a "mature and reasoned emotion which urged him": yet he "found himself compelled to use what he called the feudal terminology." Since he could not use it with the "faith and purpose" of the "feudal poets," he was "compelled to express his love a little ironically."

Given the admission that a tongue is sometimes in a cheek, the above incident looks like one of the examples. The "epiphany" —a bit of dialogue which is described as trivial—is transformed into a poem which is equally trivial.

Another private joke may lie in "epiphany" itself. It means a showing forth, a becoming manifest, especially the manifestation of Christ to the Magi. Joyce's use of this word has a many-edged purpose. The epiphany reveals the *lack* of radiance in Dublin. It points up the analogy—Joyce was always to use it—of the creative writer to God. At the same time, Joyce is poking fun at both Stephen and himself. Knowing the slightness of what the

[13]

Hero has written, he defines his goal, yet derides the steps he has taken to achieve it.

The lover of his later books would be relieved if he could think that this one has other moments where Joyce undercuts what he is nominally saying. But they are concealed: the writer's face is so straight that it is not clear where these moments are. And, even if we find them, they are merely moments. In his later works, when Joyce is equivocal, it is the conscious reflection of a philosophy. Here it is merely a correction, a secret reservation which allows him to say the pretentious things that he is saying.

In the stories, the irony is more consistent. In July, 1904, Joyce planned a group of ten. "I call the series *Dubliners* to betray the soul of that . . . paralysis which many consider a city." This sounds like one of his typical pronouncements. And—to fit what has thus far been his pattern—the early version of "The Sisters" is typically mediocre.

"Eveline" is slighter: it is rather conventional. The next, "After the Race," always failed to satisfy its writer. Then, in October, after he left with Nora, he began "Christmas Eve," dealing with one of his uncles. This he never finished; but as Richard Ellmann suggests, Joyce may have made it the basis of a story about Hallow Eve. He changed the central figure: he kept changing the title. Yet, in its final form, "Clay" is one of the good ones. Somewhere in its writing, he finally had found his tone.

He still had to wrestle with the baggage of his novel. ("This is a terrible opus: I wonder how I have the patience to write it.") The stories were congenial. In July, 1905, after "The Boarding House" and "Counterparts," he was able to say, "I am uncommonly well pleased." In September he could speak of "Ivy Day in the Committee Room" and "An Encounter" as being "very good."

[14]

He had also written "A Mother" and "A Painful Case." He had ten stories, the original number. But, by this time, he planned two more, to make a series of twelve divided into four groups: "my childhood," adolescence, maturity, and public life. The new ones, "Araby" and "Grace," were written with a sense of the position they would have in the formal structure as a whole. In addition, he revised "The Sisters," not only because it stood in need of improvement, but to make it fit the requirement of opening the book.

In the next few months, he further added "Two Gallants" to his stories of adolescence, "A Little Cloud" to those about maturity. One thing remained the same. He kept his first intention: to "betray" the city's paralysis. "There was no hope for him," the new beginning of "The Sisters"—referring to a dying priest—could just as well refer to the other people in *Dubliners.*

The stories of "my childhood" serve as an introduction. The incidents and disappointments are models of the future; the boy who tells the stories learns in his own experience what the less resilient grown-ups are to experience later. At the same time, he foreshadows the writer from whom the book is to emerge.

The use of a first-person narrator allows Joyce to do things which his usual role, that of a dispassionate observer, would not otherwise permit. When the boy tells what he thought or felt, the comment may be offered as part of the *res gestae.* At appropriate moments, he is able to speak for the writer as well as for himself. When he says there is no hope, it is with both of these voices. So, too, when this announcement is followed by a reference to paralysis: "It sounded . . . like the name of some maleficent and sinful being . . . yet I longed to be nearer . . . and look upon its deadly work."

"I saw myself as a creature driven and derided by vanity, and my eyes burned with anguish and anger." These words, the last in "Araby," last in "my childhood," precede the world of grown-ups. After this, until a similar point is reached, Joyce will intrude no comment. The anguish and anger, at least on the surface, will have to be impersonal. The sense of paralysis will have to be implicit.

The older world is divided into "adolescence" and "maturity." By adolescent Joyce means a young man or woman who has not, as yet, assumed the obligations of maturity. (In the last two stories of this group, "Two Gallants" and "The Boarding House," the characters are in their thirties. In Dublin, it would seem, adolescence is protracted.)

The stories are connected in little patterns of antithesis. Eveline, who wishes to get married, lacks the courage to go through with it, whereas in "The Boarding House," Doran does not want to but lacks the courage to resist. Eveline looks forward. ("Frank . . . would give her life.") Jimmy Doyle ("After the Race") is in the present. (He is "seeing life.")

Jimmy likes to think he's worldly: he gets befuddled and loses a lot of money at cards. The "two gallants" have the wisdom of their world. ("I know the way to get around her" and "I'm up to all their little tricks.") Corley has his triumph. Yet the other, Lenehan, as a part of his wisdom, knows what such triumphs are worth. ("Would he never get a good job . . . never have a home of his own?")

Doran has a job. At the end of "The Boarding House," he is on his way to also having a home. (He remembers "his delirium. . . . But delirium passes." "He knew that he was being had." "Once you are married you are done for.")

Doran's story is the bridge to the stories of maturity. In "A Little Cloud" and "Counterparts," we see the sort of marriage that his kind of courtship would suggest.

There is no companionship. Chandler's wife is pretty. ("Why had he married the eyes in the photograph?") After one year, he is able to realize she has "something mean" in her face. Farrington's wife ("Counterparts") is a "little sharp-faced woman" who bullies him when he is sober and is bullied when he's drunk.

Farrington aches "to rush out and revel in violence." Little Chandler is sad. (It "happened when he thought of life." "He felt how useless it was to struggle against fortune.")

"Counterparts" is followed by two tales of the unmarried. Maria (in "Clay") tries to close her eyes: everybody is "nice." In "A Painful Case," eyes are suddenly opened. Mr. Duffy is aware he is "outcast from life's feast."

Though they are divided into adolescence and maturity, these stories form a unit. In each, with one exception, there is a moment in which the character is alone with himself, a scene in which he makes a judgment on his life. The word "life" runs through the character's thought. (Life, the way of living, the routine he wants to escape: life—a heightened living—to which he is hoping to escape.) And, along with "life," words like "discontented," "embittered," and "resentful." There are occasional phrases like a "right to happiness." ("He might yet be able to . . . live happily." If he only could come across "some good simple-minded girl with a little of the ready.") But—increasingly—a sense of frustration and futility.

The exception is "Clay." But Maria's silence is a comment. When she blocks out lines about knights who "pledged their faith," suitors who sought her hand, this is a way of saying that, consciously or not, she knows what she has missed.

These eight stories, then, are a compendium of what representative Dubliners feel life has given and will give. The pretense of being an observer does not let Joyce openly announce that, in his opinion, the inhabitants of Dublin are defeated. It allows him to present a poll and, on the basis of the vote, he is able to imply what is equally depressing. A Dubliner soon begins to feel he is defeated.

In a few of the stories, the response is provoked by the events that precede it. But the events are typical: so that the feeling will recur. It may reflect the individual's age, or be colored by his temperament, yet what each of them is feeling is in the compass of the others. When he has his moment, he is speaking for all. Each is using the key suited to himself—but they are singing the same tune.

Though "A Little Cloud" stands in the middle of the book, it was the last of the fourteen stories to be written: a last chance to clarify, to get some aspect of the theme into a more telling phrase. After he meets Gallaher, Little Chandler feels, even more acutely, the disappointment of his lot. He wonders if it is too late: "It was useless, useless! He was a prisoner for life."

"Eveline" and "After the Race" do not, at first glance, show that degree of hopelessness. (The characters are young.) Nonetheless, the stories have a hidden sting. Eveline believes her life is "hard"; yet she is about to leave and, for that reason, it is not "wholly unbearable." By the end of the story, she is going to remain. Jimmy knows that morning will bring regret. He is glad of the stupor that postpones it. Yet, even while he has these thoughts, it is already "daybreak." It is later than he thinks.

In none of the stories is there a meaningful communion. The men are sociable. They are fond of song, a good phrase or anecdote—as a rule at somebody's expense. But, beyond this, neither with their women nor in the male society which takes up so much of their time is there a note of understanding or concern. Jimmy is the only one to have esteem for his companions: even then only on the level of "What jovial fellows! What good company they were!"

Each individual is conscious of what others fail to offer. No one thinks of doing or offering anything himself. (Little Chandler may occasionally have an urge to read something to his wife. Shyness holds him back: but he is ready to complain that she is too "lady-like" and "prim.") One person, Mrs. Sinico in "A Painful Case," makes a positive gesture, a slight effort to reach out. Only to be confronted by a Mr. Duffy and his inability to give.

Near the end of that story, Mr. Duffy is aware of couples in the shadows of the Park. "Venal and furtive loves" (he has not lost his habit of superiority), yet they fill him with "despair." "He felt that he was alone." The last sentence in the story, this is fittingly the last in the sampler of eight dealing with individual Dubliners. It is a thematic statement: he is speaking for all of them.

After "A Painful Case," the book moves into the areas of "public life." Politics, art, religion. The emphasis is on the group. Having already learned what a Dubliner feels, the reader is able to infer what a member of the group is feeling. Though there are indications of a similar unhappiness, these are mentioned only in passing. Individuals are seen only in terms of what they do when in the presence of others: how they act when they are bound together in some common activity—one which, supposedly, is greater than themselves.

"Ivy Day in the Committee Room" is about a group of canvassers in a municipal election. They show more interest in beer than in the candidate. Conversation keeps turning to Parnell. They are ready to be moved by verses in his memory. No one thinks to emulate his passionate commitment.

"A Mother" deals with Art. (In Dublin, this is Music.) A concert is arranged only to raise money for some cause. The quality is unimportant: one chooses artists who help to cut down the expense. The climax is a quarrel about payment of a fee.

Where the book begins with a priest who is dying, the last story, "Grace" ("The Dead" not yet written), ends with one who is aggressively alive. "A powerful-looking figure . . . crowned with a massive red face"—Father Purdon is giving a retreat.

("He won't be too hard on us." "He's a man of the world like ourselves.") Where the book began with a statement of "no hope," here is a promise of relief.

He will speak "in a businesslike way." He is "their spiritual accountant." "One thing only, he said, he would ask of his hearers . . . be straight and manly with God." If there are "discrepancies . . . be frank and say like a man . . . 'I find this wrong and this wrong. But, with God's grace, I will rectify this and this. I will set right my accounts.'"

These were the last words in the book. This is the last twist of the knife.

Many use the word "epiphany" apropos of Joyce's stories. The examples they adduce do not merit this description. There are moments of awareness. Joyce brings meaningful detail, revealing incident or phrase. But other writers do this—and without appealing to a doctrine of epiphany.

Joyce is still concerned with moments where the "whatness" of an object leaps from the "vestments" of appearance. But he also is concerned with the whatness of the vestments. The object not only has to emerge from the texture that surrounds it. It must show and establish its place within the texture.

In a letter he says that Gerhart Hauptmann's characters are "more highly vivified" than Ibsen's: yet they are "less under control. He has a difficulty in subordinating them to the action of his drama." If Joyce mentions this, it may be because the nature of his stories has made him especially conscious of this need for "control." He will try to vivify. But, if he is going to present a world of shabbiness, he must limit the amount of color, of stature and intensity.

The style that he uses is one of "scrupulous meanness." There is an "odour of ashpits and old weeds and offal [that] hangs around my stories." Phrases about paralysis, loneliness, or futility are realistic details. (What the people think.) They take their place with similar details: dusty cretonne, rinds of bacon, a stove that has grown cold, a shave that is not taken, an uninhabited house in the blind end of a street.

The incidents are commonplace. Not only are his people "subordinate" to action: action is subordinate to the flatness that prevails.

In the last few stories there are the beginnings of a change. Gallaher ("A Little Cloud") shows a bit of color. But we know that Joyce thought him a type of Oliver Gogarty. If we compare him to a later type—Buck Mulligan in *Ulysses*—we can see how much of the flamboyance has been muted.

An article has tried to show that the stories as a whole reflect what happens in the *Odyssey*. A second finds a system of Christian virtues and sins, while other essays have perceived Elijah in "A Little Cloud," the Virgin Mary in "Clay." Joyce's brother Stanislaus, denying the presence of these or any parallels, offers his own contribution. His brother let him know that "Grace" is a burlesque of *The Divine Comedy*.

But, in saying this, Stanislaus gives sanction to the others. Dante took people from the classical world and scriptures. Most of all, people from his native city. Joyce uses Dante as his model, but does not have a hundred cantos: so that his characters play on many stages at one time. The incidents are not only naturalistic. Many are allusions to both Bible and *Odyssey*—as well as to incidents in Dante. In "The Holy Office," Joyce mentions Dante by name (with Aristotle and Aquinas) as one of his masters. When he writes:

To enter heaven, travel hell,

Joyce is thinking of his stories.

What he wants to show is implicit in all of them. But he needs a model which will show him how to subdivide, will tell him how —and where—to allocate the aspects of "paralysis."

When he began "The Sisters," Joyce did not have all of his plots in mind. (The one for "The Boarding House" came to him only in Trieste.) But his model, his consort of models, would tell him what to look for. It gave a hint for incidents, for details of description or of speech.

The scheme of parallels is not evenly applied. (Nor is it in *Ulysses*.) They are in the nature of check-points on his route. He may linger: or merely touch and run.

Many of the correspondences seem far-fetched or trivial. Even then, they give a basis for comparison. He must put each episode in the same framework as its model before he is able to show how they differ. It is the contrast that is important. The situation is similar, but where Odysseus acts, the Dubliner does not. Where Odysseus wins, the Dubliner loses. Homer's hero escapes, the other is caught. When Little Chandler is becalmed, he finds that Gallaher (Aeolus) does not bring a sail-filling wind. On the biblical level, Gallaher (Elijah) does not bring a fructifying rain.

In the parallels to Dante, the difference is one of scale. After all, the Dubliners have committed the same sins. But, in this town, even hell is petty. The sin and sinners are diminished.

In the early stories, analogies are simple. Eveline—little Eve—does not leave the Garden. A few sketchy details show a correspondence. But, as the scheme evolves, the analogies are more complex. In a late story like "Two Gallants," Joyce has to make them fit those he already has used.

For instance, "Eveline" is an example of Prudence. Jimmy ("After the Race") exemplifies its lack. (In Dublin, presence of a Virtue is no better than its absence.) "The Boarding House" shows a lack of Fortitude. Joyce wrote "Two Gallants" to deal with its presence.

The Hero is divided: the lion and the fox. On the biblical level, Joyce takes Judges as the model. Many of the details, including

[22]

some of the oddest, are suggested by its pages. (Corley is Samson: he is "too hairy." Lenehan — as Samson — has a stock of riddles.) Judges gives the writer a large number of incidents. He can choose the ones he thinks most appropriate. But, once again, it's the difference that is important. Gideon refuses the crown: Corley asks for a half-sovereign.

On the Homeric level, Joyce is more restricted. In a book of weakness, this episode must show a hero who is strong and resourceful. He takes the story of the Cyclops. Corley has Odysseus' muscle. Lenehan has the "adroitness."

But, in this town, its heroes are like Cyclops:

> A race of proud-liv'd loiterers,
> None for another caring.

In a "white sailor hat," the girl is Odysseus. She does not escape the Cyclops.

The Dantean level brings still another problem. Jimmy and his friends are in the First Circle. (The Virtuous Pagans.) The lovers in "The Boarding House" are in the Second Circle. (The subject is Lust.) So when Joyce decides on a story to be placed between them, there is too much that has already been used. Instead of the abundance Judges or the Cyclops gave him, he must make do with only a few items.

They are at the beginning of the story. The description of the "carnal sinners" is present, if disguised, in his opening paragraph. (The "living texture below . . . changing shape and hue unceasingly . . . sent into the air an unchanging, unceasing murmur.") He also gives Corley a few traits of Minos. After this, only the subject is similar: Lust and, by inference, the quality of Dublin's Love.

Joyce uses the symbolic figure of a harp. "Heedless that her covering had fallen about her knees," it "seemed weary alike of the eyes of strangers and of her master's hands. One hand played in the bass the melody of *Silent, O Moyle*." The relevant verse is not mentioned. "Still in her darkness doth Erin lie sleeping."

Joyce has placed the scene near the National Library and National Museum. But the harp is also Corley's slavey. She, too, is "Lir's loneliest daughter"—both as individual and as symbol of the girls of Dublin. She, too, quiescent, lies sleeping in her darkness.

"The Boarding House," by contrast, has the woman as aggressor. Not because of ardor. The body is passive. But sex is a commodity to barter. If she uses it correctly, Polly may be able (with the aid of her mother) to trade it up into marriage.

At this time, Joyce got back to "The Sisters." Once the other stories grew so related to their models, he was obliged to show that this story was the place where each particular chain of correspondences began.

The Bible had been preempted: he had dealt with Eve. The solution is ingenious. "In the beginning was the Word." He adds the word *paralysis.* Indeed, a trinity of words. *Simony* is worldly traffic in spiritual things. *Gnomon* is the remnant of a parallelogram left when a smaller but similar part of the parallelogram is missing. Father, Holy Spirit, Son. The Father is paralyzed. The Holy Spirit is debased. The Son—hope of renewal—is missing.

These three words are the Three Beasts of Dante. On the Homeric level, the Father does not survive: the boy will not seek him. In the next story, "An Encounter," the boy meets Nestor. Dante meets Virgil. The "josser" who is an advocate of punishment is the embodiment of Charity.

Joyce has been a presence in these stories. (Another of the patterns which he found in Dante.) The question in "Eveline"—whether to leave the country—is one he was considering at the time of writing. With a dead mother, an overbearing father, the

[24]

oldest daughter, Poppie, attending to the house and small children, the Joyce family was similar to that in the story. Poppie was trying to dissuade him: yet with the insight that his need to escape was equally hers, Joyce took Poppie as a surrogate for himself, then used Eveline as a surrogate for both. (Notice that the suitor calls Eveline "Poppens.")

So, too, some of Jimmy's friends have the names of people whom Joyce knew in Paris. Jimmy, who is ready to see them as exemplars of cosmopolitan grace, is a type of Joyce, a parody of Joyce's feeling for foreign writers he admires. Like Jimmy, he is elated by the speed of their vehicle: beguiled by the thought of a common venture. (They are in a car that is "careering.")

Jimmy, "who mistook his cards," only succeeds in losing ("How much had he written away?") a large part of the riches he had "at his disposal."

These two stories, then, written while Joyce was thinking of leaving with Nora, are admonitions to himself. Do not stay in Dublin. But—don't mistake your cards. Don't give up your heritage. Your subject is Ireland.

The stories Joyce wrote in Trieste are also cautionary tales. But the parables are used for purposes of reassurance. They are in a curious subjunctive: he is looking into the future. If I had stayed in Dublin, this is what I might be when thirty or forty: Doran, who in youth had "denied the existence of God" and otherwise "sown his wild oats"—"for nine tenths of the year [he leads] a regular life," meaning that he finds release in a protracted annual bender. Lenehan, who makes use of "eloquence" and knowledge—stories, riddles, limericks—only in order to cadge drinks . . .

In a letter to Stanislaus (July, 1905), Joyce insists that his "experiment"—leaving Ireland with Nora—has not been a failure. He has "begotten a child": he has kept a job. Meanwhile,

[25]

in his writing, he has produced a body of work of commendable quality and quantity. "I do not think that I have wasted my time." In the stories, Joyce gives a similar answer to himself.

The letter also refers to his relationship to Nora. He feels sorry about the poverty he is inflicting. Moreover—"With one entire side of my nature, she has no sympathy." She is always crying.

But he has finished "The Boarding House." A study of a typical marriage in Dublin—what it means to the participants and how it is achieved—the story is a latent comment on his particular union. It is an answer to the worry in himself.

Doran's fate might have easily been his. He would be unable to resist the lure of sensuality: he would be too weak when marriage is demanded. But, instead of this, he and Nora have a relationship that they entered of their own free will.

Polly (like Nora) has a drunken father. She uses phrases like *I seen*. "But," Doran thinks, "what would grammar matter if he really loved her?" In the case of Joyce, there is love between them. Grammar does not matter.

In some of the stories, there is no occasion for a similarly deep involvement; yet, to some degree, there is always some relevant personal allusion. In the two stories he wrote before "The Dead," Joyce gets back to the topics in the letter. If he had stayed in Dublin, he would have been like Lenehan. (Even in Trieste, he is a bit of a cadger.) Yet, by making the suggestion, by this overstatement, he is able to refute the charge. He may not be a conscientious worker. And yet—as he said to Stanislaus—he has continued to work. One way or another, he has managed to support his family.

So, too, with Little Chandler: a person he could almost be, a person that he isn't. (On one hand, self-indictment. On the other, justification.) Chandler envies the successes of people who are coarser. He imagines the attention he will get with his poems:

he phrases some of the reviews. But the reader knows that he will not write the poems.

Joyce is not fond of his verses: yet he has written them. And, by this story, he shows he is capable of something more. "A page of *A Little Cloud* gives me more pleasure," he said, "than all my verses." (There is another item of self-congratulation. Little Chandler yearns for the passion he is not able to get from a wife who is too proper.)

The stories are self-sufficient, written to be read without knowledge of parallels. Indeed, such knowledge may spoil them. One becomes too conscious of identifications. What was unassuming seems busy and contrived.

Under the concealment of his "scrupulous meanness," Joyce has been able to indulge the prankish side of his nature. God is a Father or Employer. Thus, when Eveline is Eve, Mr. Hill is angry, jealous, full of hate for foreigners. (He is bad on Saturday.) Jimmy's father used to be a nationalist butcher. After opening some branches—becoming "a merchant prince"—he has "modified his views." In "Counterparts," it's rumored that Mr. Alleyne (El) is "sweet" on Miss Delacour. (Affable, plump, middle-aged, she has a "Jewish appearance.") One may smile or shudder. But, even when they are good, the quips go against the grain of what Joyce is writing. As he said himself, he is "too mischievous."

At the same time, he is too portentous. The stories are too slight for a many-leveled structure. The voice Joyce has muted is not able to sustain the would-be thunder of his wrath. It almost seems like a parody of those medieval storybooks where each anecdote is followed by a *moraliter* or *mistice*.

He intended *Dubliners* as a "chapter in the moral history of my country"—a "first step towards" its "spiritual liberation." Even so, he felt he was "unnecessarily harsh." There was a gaiety in Dublin, a genial hospitality, to which he had not done justice.

Joyce was not a Dante: his humors were too volatile. He could not maintain that grave consistency of tone. In the future, he would tailor his work more closely to himself. He was going to let in the playfulness which, as a matter of fact, he was not able to keep out. But, from now on, it would be a part of the design.

But he had to finish *Dubliners*. Though the scheme of fourteen stories was complete, some of the parallels had not been brought to their conclusion. While Joyce was having troubles with publisher and printer, he had time to add a coda, a new story, "The Dead," in which he could put his second thoughts into effect; say things he should have said—say them in a different way—meanwhile taking the parallels to a fitting *terminus ad quem*.

He had learned to work on a more elaborate scale. "The Dead" opens with a party—the longest scene in the book. Thus far, the story is not appreciably better than what has gone before. What transfigures it is the episode which follows.

The scene has narrowed: a married couple is alone. Gretta tells her husband of a suitor she once had. He is dead, but Gabriel sees that the other, Michael, still has meaning in her life.

Up to the scene in the hotel-room, the life in each of the stories has been measured out by the writer. He has kept the reader—as he has kept himself—at a distance from what happens. But, after the long description of the party, "The Dead" suddenly breaks out. There is a deeper, more autonomous vitality. The reader is drawn into the room.

What Gretta tells her husband is related to an episode in the life of Nora. This biographical aspect is not an end in itself. That the incident had happened made the material available. As a writer, Joyce might use it, but only when it is the proper material to use. It had to earn its way. It must play a part in his parallels: it must be consistent with his attitude to Dublin. For once in these stories, he tries to show the contrast that has always been implicit. As opposed to the thin activities of Dublin, "the full glory of some passion."

One may marvel at the skill with which so many parallels have been gathered into an expression of emotion. We have a congeries of endings. The time is one of festivity—as it was in Ithaca. Gabriel is confronted with the problem of Odysseus. A young man is taking what is rightfully the husband's.

It is Christmas season. "The Dead" opens with an echo of the Annunciation. It ends with Michael's graveyard. "Crosses . . . spears" and "thorns": an echo of the Crucifixion. The last few words take one even further—to the "last end" when Christ delivers judgment on "the living and the dead."

Gabriel is the angel of the Annunciation and Last Trumpet. ("The Dead" is framed between them.) Michael is the angel of the loss of Eden. In Gretta's memory he merges with the youthful Adam. ("A person long ago"—"at the end of the garden"— "there was a tree.") He has not aged. Gretta is older. She is the second Eve—the other Mother of us All. He has become her Son. ("Isn't it a terrible thing to die as young as that?" "I was great with him," she says.)

On another level, we are in the *Paradiso*. The vision of falling snow is the Beatific Vision. The moment that precedes it is the Invocation to the Virgin. The "generous tears" fill Gabriel's eyes. They come because of Gretta. In evoking them, she plays the part of Mary, intercessor for humanity.

The writer listens to her pleading. He has his view of Irish religiosity; yet he gives a moment to the yearning which is present.

She is Humanity. She is the people of Ireland. Though her days are occupied with other things, she keeps a thought of Love —a thought of Christ. ("I think he died for me.")

The story is related to two Joyce wrote in the summer of 1905

[29]

("Ivy Day," "A Painful Case"). In "The Dead," he puts the theme, the dominion of passion and the past, into a larger perspective.

Gabriel sees that Michael—in his love—felt something he himself has not been able to experience. He is not resentful. ("It hardly pained him to think how poor a part he, her husband, had played in her life.") In *Ulysses,* Bloom, having many rivals, sees them as part of a series. Gabriel sees his as part of a dialogue. Michael, all the dead, he himself, like all the living ("one by one . . . becoming shades"), are comprehended in a process. Michael, in his feeling, he, in contemplation, are brothers in the fact and implication of mortality.

The unequivocal tone has become equivocal. As in the later books, there is a balance of reciprocal forces. Each loses on one level—and triumphs on the other. What Michael did is foolish: but he is remembered. So with the youthful heroes, romantic, self-destructive, who fill the history of Ireland. So, too, with the youthful Christ. In each case, the past reaches into the present. The memory of what is dead may inhibit one's pleasure in the living. Even so, it brings a sense of something richer— gives the heart a consciousness that it would not otherwise have had.

Michael's symbol is traditionally snow. That of Gabriel is fire. "The flakes . . . [are] falling obliquely against the lamplight." What Michael has to offer is necessarily transient. Yet, as the story ends, it is snow that is active. Beyond the confines of his window, the purview of his lamp, Gabriel can see it, hear it— "falling softly" over Ireland, "falling faintly through the universe."

That it will melt is a thing we know. Stopping where he does, Joyce has counterpoised the feeling and the knowledge. There is an echo of Dante. In the last canto of the *Paradiso*—the last canto of the *Divine Comedy*—"My vision almost wholly fades, and still there drops within my heart the sweetness that was born of it. Thus the snow loses its imprint in the sun."

The reader, as a rule, is not aware of this supplementary material. He sees only the naturalistic level. But this level is enough. As in the other stories, it provides a simpler and, to many tastes, more desirable form of what Joyce is trying to express. In "The Dead," the statement is complex. Even in this simple form, it is not easy to express.

In the other stories, the theme was one of paralysis. The texture was consistent. No matter where we stopped, we found confirmation of the deprivation and arrest. The only movement was in the narrative itself. When this was completed, we had learned nothing that was not implicit in the early paragraphs.

In "The Dead," Joyce has broken and recast the mold. The world of constant figures has become one of forces that, in relation to each other, vary in dimension and direction. At the end we get a resultant of components that were introduced at different periods of time. If we stop before this, we get a smaller spectrum, a different resultant — not the statement that Joyce will finally convey.

The account of the party is his amends to Dublin. There are images of obsolescence, images of death remembered, anticipated, or deferred. Nonetheless, Gabriel can feel that the people who are there have qualities of kindly humor, humanity, and hospitality that belonged to a more spacious day. This is not the theme that is finally presented, but it sets up a reservoir of loving-kindness on which the author will draw later.

Though he may not consciously recall it, the reader will be affected by what has gone before. The leisurely events lead to Gretta's memory of Michael. The story changes key. The pathos that death brings turns into the pain. Yet what we have read, like a sustaining pedal, keeps a note of tenderness to play against and with the notes that are being played.

[31]

The party, the hotel-room, the meditation after Gretta is asleep—the story, in effect, is a series of movements which keep diminishing in size. In each, the treatment changes: the cast of characters gets smaller. At the same time, the frame of reference is enlarged. Itself a postscript to the other stories, "The Dead" is constructed like a chain of postscripts. Each modifies the body of the letter, becomes part of the letter, then—with it—is modified by the codicil which follows.

In the final paragraph, there is no human character, yet the range has been extended till it includes the universe. The sense is created by extralogical means: by the rhythm, the sound, the effect of the diminution and extension, by the visual effect of the falling snow, by the hidden weight of unobtrusive phrases ("lonely churchyard," "dark, mutinous . . . waves"), by the increment, the resonance, the many kinds of resonance the moment has inherited.

The essays, in general, had a uniform style. Joyce used another in his songs, another in the stories. In each mode he showed a different aspect of himself, a different part of his equipment. Now in "The Dead," with its contradictory phases, its paradoxical statement, he began to bring together a few of the tools he had separately sharpened.

This may have been required by the particular occasion: yet, having learned the method, Joyce was never to leave it. It reflected something in himself. At his best, his work is like an Irish stew. (He used this image in the *Wake*.) If he leaves out some of the ingredients, it is incomplete: too skimpy or too dry. A denatured Joyce. He needs the unity, the variation of textures, interpenetration of juices. Not only is the dish enhanced, but the separate ingredient, while remaining itself, gains a virtue from the others.

The end of "The Dead" is close to being "fine writing." But, in its context, its position—the tip of an inverted pyramid, bearing, balancing the story that precedes it—this is poetry more moving than what is offered in the poems. (The scene in the hotel-room is a more dramatic scene than any in *Exiles*.) He had learned that, tacking, changing direction, he was able to reach destinations that were otherwise inaccessible.

Gabriel is writing reviews for the *Daily Express*. (Just like Joyce himself in 1902–3.) Pedantic, heavy in personal relations, never suspecting that Gretta might have memories, he is a projection. If Joyce had married Nora, if they had stayed in Dublin . . . Yet the scene in the hotel-room (as it does with everything) takes both Gabriel and Joyce into a new dimension.

In the two previous stories, Joyce dealt with the theme of contrasting types. Chandler or Lenehan—reflective doubles of himself—are opposed to a more active companion. "The Dead" presents a higher form of this polarity. If Michael is a version of Gallaher or Corley, he is a version that is radiant. They are envied their successes—whatever these are worth. Gabriel envies Michael his defeat, the implications of his death. ("Better pass boldly . . . in the full glory of some passion, than . . . wither dismally with age.")

"The time had come to set out on his journey westward." (On the other coast—a half-mythical region where, in almost-legendary time, Michael came to Gretta in the garden—Galway is the antithesis to the aridity of Dublin.)

Joyce had heard the incident on which this story is based when he first met Nora. To him, the information was not the shock that it would be to Gabriel after years of marriage. If there were to be any changes, they would come later; they would be due to the continuing relationship. So when Gabriel feels a new awareness, he is putting into a single moment what Joyce, in gradual fashion, has increasingly been feeling. It happens too quickly. The change is too abrupt to be an accurate image for a deepening in Joyce. It is more relevant to his growing as a writer.

[33]

This story, the last to be written, is the last story in the book: a good time and place for a proclamation. The writing of "The Dead" is Joyce's new experience. It is as a writer that he is going to Galway! He is Odysseus who, at the end of *his* book, says, "There lies before me a great and hazardous adventure, which I must see through to the end however far this may be." He is Ulysses who, from a flame in the *Inferno*, says, "Not fondness for a son, duty to an aged father, nor the love I owed Penelope . . . could conquer within me the passion I had to gain experience of the world and of the vices and worth of men. . . . [I passed that] outlet where Hercules set up his landmarks so that men should not pass beyond."

We may be sure that, at this time, Joyce was not able to envisage the precise latitude to which his voyage would take him. If he had thoughts about Bloom and Molly, they were still vague. As for *Finnegans Wake* . . . But he knew what would be his first reach. He "would rewrite *Stephen Hero* completely."

The revision is doubly a voyage. On one level, Joyce is the sailor. On another, it is Stephen. The words of Ulysses prefigure his education in "vices and worth." They look forward to his consciousness of Hell: to his realization that experience is an antecedent to his art. They point to the moment when Stephen recognizes that his own priesthood is that of the artist. ("To live, to err, to fall, to triumph, to recreate life out of life!")

A Portrait of the Artist is a hard book to evaluate with objectivity. A quest for identity is part of a reader's experience. But, at different times, the specific problems take a different form. Religion, family, and sex have a different relevance. As he grows older, a reader's own attitude to his youth may vary. He tends to judge the book in terms of his empathy with Stephen at the time of his reading.

One who writes about *A Portrait* has an additional impediment. In the last chapter, Stephen offers his discourse on aesthetics. It is often taken as a definitive statement of Joyce's credo and intent, but the structure of the book is dislocated by this emphasis. (*A Portrait* was not written to give Joyce an occasion to make that famous remark about God and his fingernails.)

The Artist in the title is a particular artist. He is also the archetypical artist. No matter how individual the young Stephen may be, he is a member of a class. There are incidents that indicate a time and place or Stephen's personality. Yet what is shown has to be equivalent to what happens to others. Nothing is offered just because it happened to Joyce or he thought it a nice touch to put into his portrait.

It is said *A Portrait* lacks the fullness of *Stephen Hero*. This is like saying a boat lacks the fullness of the log from which it has been hollowed.

In the University, Joyce, like many students, had discussions with friends. In each of the versions, Stephen also has them. They develop topics which are important to the book. They give Stephen a chance to explain himself. He has found associates with whom he has an interest, a turn of mind or temperament in common. The nature of the similarity—its extent and limitations—helps to define him further.

Among the people in whom Joyce confided, there was his brother Stanislaus. As Maurice, he is prominent in *Stephen Hero*. In *A Portrait,* Joyce is more schematic. Stephen's classmates, Davin, Lynch, or Cranly, are able to assimilate all he may say to Maurice. (Each occupies a different area of Stephen's conversation.) Despite the prominence of "Maurice" in life or the early version, Joyce reduces his role.

Joyce's brother George died in 1902. His death served as the basis of the scenes in *Stephen Hero* that concern the death of Isabel. Yet Joyce felt these scenes should be distinct from the discussions. He changed the time of death: put it in the summer-vacation where he was able to deal with it in isolation. In the new version, he was able to dismiss it. No matter what it meant to the artist as individual, in a study of the archetype the death is a digression.

It is true, then, that this new version is sparser. But the other is crowded. By his having thinned it, Joyce has given what remained an opportunity to bloom. The color is less neutral: the outlines are more sharp. He has started to luxuriate in his new liberty to work in different styles, to practice various skills.

The characters (those he has retained) have more presence than in *Stephen Hero*. They have more than the people in *Dubliners*. In the latter, they are molecules of Dublin. The town being drab, they share in its drabness. Here they are presented as a part of the environment of a fellow who is remarkable. They catch some of the glow he radiates. The people in *Stephen* are the notes for characters to be created. In the stories, they are seen through the wrong end of a telescope: alive but tinier than life. In *A Portrait,* even the lowliest is in the court of Charlemagne or Arthur.

In "The Sisters" and "Araby," Joyce introduced his father as the anonymous uncle. In *A Portrait,* Simon is not the explosive person that he will be in *Ulysses.* But he has begun to sputter. Joyce will always keep his people under his control: yet he is learning how to give more liberty even while he holds them to his pattern.

The incidents are filtered through the sensibilities of Stephen. They become alive only when he touches them: lapse back into darkness when this animation is removed.

What he feels is shown by the evocation of his moods. They are those of an impressionable boy, of an even more impressionable adolescent, of a poetaster near the turn of the century. Joyce always had a tendency to indulge in "swooning" passages.

In the stories, he was restricted by the "meanness." Here he has the excuse that the tone-poem is proper to a "poet."

In *Ulysses,* the scented paragraphs are shorter. The soft phrases are in immediate contact with a jagged edge of mockery. In *A Portrait,* where everything is presented as it appears to Stephen, a reader may not notice that the sentiments expressed are not necessarily Joyce's. At the end of the fourth chapter, when Stephen suddenly knows that he will be a writer, one is conquered by the mood. In a moment of less intensity, when a reader is capable of more detachment, this swooning may remind him of a narcissistic fiddler who, his eyes closed, is playing a Romantic piece.

In the early chapters, Stephen is a sensorium. He is acted on. In the last, he begins to polish his remarks to others. They are not always wise — but they have a crackle, an economy, and bite that Joyce had shown only in "The Holy Office." He improves on that. There he set himself the task of saying something smart of each writer that he mentioned. He stopped as soon as he ran out of writers or good phrases. Here each of the phrases, in addition to its value as an epigram, has to tell us something about Stephen. There is a reason for its being in the book.

In one aspect, Joyce is less free than he was in *Dubliners.* There he selected incidents, from his life or elsewhere, because he found them suitable to the uses he intended. Here he starts with the material. Though he gives it shape, it must be a shape to which this material consents.

There is also the hold of *Stephen Hero.* While he tries to judge how much he can throw away, Joyce also tries to see how much he may salvage. He retains some incidents which, if he started from scratch, he would not have put into the book. In the phrase he uses in describing Cranly — "by an act of will he tried to make [them] significant."

Joyce also had to forego the aid parallels gave him. In the stories, they were a standard against which the incidents were measured. In Dublin, such is the wisdom of Nestor, such are Paolo and Francesca or the exploits of Elijah. In *A Portrait*, there is no lack of analogues. Inevitably there will be a reference to Ovid's Dedalus. There is an implicit reference to Odysseus. There are other voyages, other stories of apprenticeship. But the point they make is never one of contrast. They enrich the texture; but the only comment they make is that other people have had a similar experience.

Stephen has to do what a young man does. A young man as artist: or artist as a young man. ("I go to encounter for the millionth time the reality of experience.")

The structure of the book is that of a schedule. Richard Ellmann sees an embryo "in the process of gestation." It "begins with Stephen's father" and, just before the end, shows "severance from his mother." The first chapter has "the soul . . . surrounded by liquids, urine, slime, seawater, amniotic tides"; later, "fully developed, fattening itself for its journey . . . it is ready to leave."

This is the point where Hugh Kenner begins. He sees the early pages as "Aristotelian catalogue . . . senses, faculties and mental activities . . . counterpointed against the unfolding of the infant conscience." Sidney Feshbach charts the "traditional progression called . . . 'the ladder of perfection' . . . vegetative, animal, rational, angelic and divine."

There are other patterns. Sages have described the phases of Man's recurring voyage. Joyce has included details so that Stephen's voyage tallies with each of the descriptions. This helps to organize the sequence of chapters. Yet frequently these details have only a symbolic value. If Stephen sees a ditch, this fact has little interest. It acquires emphasis and color only when Ellmann shows that such a ditch is related to amniotic fluids.

[38]

That Stephen passes a milestone is certainly significant. The event, in theory, has behind it the weight of millions who have done so. In practice, these occasions have a tendency to be perfunctory—like a high-school graduation.

If the book has body, it is primarily because this has been provided by the set-pieces which, though thematic, are not part of these systems. The first chapter, for example, has the Christmas dinner. The third has the sermon about Hell.

In 1908, after writing this chapter, Joyce stopped work on *A Portrait*. One year later he tried to form a chain of cinemas in Ireland. In Dublin, Vincent Cosgrave, Lynch in *Stephen Hero*, told him he had been intimate with Nora. Others were able to persuade him that Cosgrave was lying. Nonetheless, he was never able to forget the period when he had doubted.

The incident is crucial to his later books. His play *Exiles* touches on infidelity. But the next steps are more particularly his. In *Ulysses* and *Finnegans Wake*, he will make the incident more culpable: broaden it, turn it to burlesque: turn it into a universal. This may be a method of defense, a way of distancing pain. Yet each man builds his defenses with the material he has at hand. This material, these tendencies, were Joyce's.

These books came later. He had to finish *A Portrait*. In the two chapters that he wrote when he returned, it is hard to see a trace of the disturbance. Compared to *Stephen Hero*, there are changes in the role of Lynch. But these are not the ones we might have expected. There are good, impersonal reasons for making them. And, in some ways, both the role and its meaning are enhanced.

In the fourth chapter, Stephen realizes that he will be an artist. Like the embryo who, from the first, is fated to become a man, he must nonetheless pass through phases that are indeterminate before he finally reaches a point of definition. "Restless moodiness," "vague dissatisfaction"—these are aspects of

[39]

adolescence and a consciousness of sex. A sense of being "different," of "a great part which he felt awaited him"—these are also typical. It is only later that they will take on the appearance of the artist's discontent.

Stephen has a love of language. In school, he has a "reputation" for essays. These are hints: yet not necessarily the sign of a writer who is preordained. (The morning after the discussion at the Christmas dinner, he tries to write about Parnell—but "his brain . . . refused to grapple with the theme.")

The little incidents, the phrases scattered through the early chapters, are like iron filings. As if in answer to a magnet, after Stephen's self-determination they leap into a pattern, the contour of his field of force.

He will be a writer . . . This is the one moment of transition when the rites that celebrate it have the elevation that is commensurate to it. That does not make him Joyce. He is merely the Stephen who was mentioned and described in the beginning of this essay.

Joyce was now the father of two children: close to being Bloom. As for writing, he would always have his intervals of doubt. But as opposed to Stephen, he was the author of "Ivy Day," "Two Gallants," and "The Dead."

Looking back on Stephen, Joyce has to be ambivalent. Stephen is inferior. Yet this early self has within it the seed of everything that Joyce in his most arrogant mood may have thought about himself. In the fifth and final chapter, there is a double irony. Stephen, who, to hear him speak, is striding into Life—isn't he the silly fellow? And this silly, touchy, ungainly, insecure, self-centered posturing fellow—this is the little frog that (wait, give him a chance) is going to become a prince.

If Joyce offers comment, it is through the incidents he chooses. In the first chapter, we have the story of Father Dolan and the pandybat. The emphasis it gets shows the importance that it

[40]

has for Stephen. "That was cruel and unfair." Yet, three chapters later, he remembers that, in all his years at school, he "re-
ceived only two pandies and, though these had been dealt him in
the wrong, he knew that he had often escaped punishment." It
still is "cruel" and "unfair"—but on a different scale, in a different perspective.

Like his schoolboy self, Stephen is going to protect his dignity.
He has cause to do so. And yet—now as then—his picture of his
world, though in many ways true, is not necessarily gospel.

In the second chapter, he is shown as "angry with himself for
being young and the prey of restless foolish impulses." He would
dream that "he would be transfigured. . . . Weakness and
timidity and inexperience would fall from him in that magic
moment." He "tried to build a breakwater . . . against the sordid
tide of life without him and to dam up . . . [the] recurrence of the
tides within."

In the arms of his first whore, Stephen finds a modulation of
the "magic moment" of his dream: she is a modulation of the
figure in his dream. "Her room was warm and lightsome."
"Proud . . . movements of her perfumed head." She "embraced
him gaily and gravely." "Her face . . . in serious calm." This is
not the stuff of which *Dubliners* is made.

"He felt that he had suddenly become strong and fearless and
sure of himself." This is a fantastification. It is like his picture of
the whore.

This experience—this new way of life—is not the end of tur-
moils. (The haven that it offers is the cause of some of them.)
Though he has been translated to a different mode, the qualities of weakness have been translated with him. He is still looking for a barrier against the tide. But the strength he seeks is not
entirely positive. He is looking for an absence—absence of not
being fearless, of not being strong.

Now, chapters later, he is going to be an artist. This is the high point of the book. Seeing it through Stephen's eyes, the reader has to feel, as he is meant to do, Stephen's exultation and triumph. Yet the underside is present. The moment is a modulation of the moment with the whore and of Stephen's dream.

He "wanted to meet in the real world the unsubstantial image which his soul so consciously beheld." He adapted the whore to this desire. The girl he sees on the beach is related to both. (Like a "beautiful seabird," "without shame or wantonness.") Once again, he is seeing what he has been predisposed to see.

There has been a progression. The boyhood dream was passive. (The encounter would result "without any overt act.") He became more active. Of his own volition ("Onward, undismayed"), he went into the brothel area. Yet he "would not bend to kiss her." The woman "bowed his head." ("It was too much for him. He closed his eyes surrendering himself to her.")

In this new scene, it is the girl who is passive: she "whom magic had changed." "On and on . . . he strode . . . singing wildly to the sea." Even so, there is an aspect of submission. ("His soul" is "swooning into some new world, fantastic, dim, uncertain.")

The wholeness, harmony, and radiance that Stephen sees in art are not present in his work. (He has nominated himself, but he is not yet one of the elect.) They are not present in his life. He has problems that he has not solved—plus the new ones added by his new commitment.

In the last chapter, he projects an image of assurance. He persuades his audience. (Joyce persuades the reader.) His doubts are not readily apparent. "A tide began to surge beneath the calm surface of [his] friendliness." He speaks with "cold violence." Yet, because of misdirection, we overlook the violence. We remember the coldness and the "calm."

Stephen's words have gained a more decisive eloquence. They give the book a glitter. "Silence, exile and cunning." Nationality, language, religion. I shall try to fly by these nets." Yet for all his "silence," he is spilling his heart—even telling of his "private life" to the unlikely Davin, who is so dismayed that he is not able to eat dinner.

Stephen is not averse to "nationality" per se. As he tells Cranly, he is not sure that "religion" is false. (He is clearly not forgoing his love of hymns or his admiration for Aquinas.) What he means is this: I would be an artist. I will try to fly by the aspects of religion or nationality that interfere with my being one.

As for "language"—in the care he uses, Stephen shows his appreciation, as well as his allegiance. (One may say that with "language" or "silence" what Stephen has in mind is not their usual sense. But, in these slogans, the words are resonant because of the meaning that they seem to have. The meaning that they have in "the market place.")

In his lectures in Trieste, Joyce had already shown a love of country. In "The Dead," a tolerance to Dublin. Nationality, language, and religion are a subject of his art. It may be that in the statement which he gives to Stephen he has included a hidden comment by himself. It has been noticed that, in this sentence, the word "by" is ambiguous. Stephen says that he will try to fly *past*. But the writer knows that he himself is flying *by means of* these particular nets. And, in this sense, "nets" is also ambiguous. To the aerial "artist," they are the things that give him his security.

The set-piece in the final chapter is the discourse on aesthetics, a consolidation and revision of passages in *Stephen Hero*. This section has been treated as a declaration of Joyce's present, past, and even future credo. But it is hard to believe that, in order to supply such a declaration, Joyce put an interlude, like a roadblock, into his novel. This scene must have a novelistic function.

It shows that Stephen is thinking about art: it shows he has skill in phrasing and ordering his thought. In a covert way, it shows that his shining edifice of art is also an escape. When he thinks of going into the unknown, a part of him is thinking of the tempest that he leaves behind.

He must seem "indifferent." The impression is supported by the impersonality of his recourse to Aquinas. His cool, timeless edifice is in a different universe from the one in which he hopes to live, to err, fall, and triumph. It is possible to reconcile them. Yet, in this scene, it is only the cool tower of art which is manifest.

Instead of the abrasive Stephen, this one is serene, a scholar and saint of art, generous in passing wisdom to an errable disciple. As a lecturer he uses pauses, changes in his pace or tone, quotation, rhetorical question, vivid illustration, the detour only to return. And, in his capacity as writer, Joyce adds stage-directions, pictures of the city landscape or an interruption by a student who, to set off Stephen, makes superficial remarks on the subject of aesthetics.

Lynch has a complex part. First he is the audience. He has sensitivities: these pay tribute to Stephen. Second, he is a contrast. Unlike the patient Stephen, he keeps losing his temper. He curls his lip, grimaces, whinnies, rubs his groin. Where Stephen carefully composes long, exalted cadences, he uses interjections. ("'Bull's eye again!' said Lynch wittily.")

Lest a reader feel that Stephen's system of order is a response to his personal condition, Lynch serves as a scapegoat. The disabilities are diverted to his shoulders. Stephen has no money, but he offers a cigarette to Lynch. "I know you are poor." "Damn your yellow insolence," says Lynch. But he takes —even the last one. The idea that poverty is a factor in Stephen's theories is effectively removed. The poverty belongs to Lynch.

Do we think it incongruous that a carnal Stephen should speak of disembodied Beauty? This is also diverted. "Remember,"

[44]

says Lynch, "though I did eat a cake of cowdung once, that I admire only beauty." Stephen raises "his cap as if in greeting." He, too, so to speak, has dabbled in cowdung. But as applied to Stephen this is only a figure of speech. "We are all animals," he says. "I also am an animal." But, in context, he is merely showing he is kind.

Most important, Lynch is a mouthpiece. Not only for the writer: he also speaks for Stephen. There are various comments that Stephen does not care to make—not even to himself. These are externalized. It is Lynch who makes them. Stephen's own doubts are on the lips of a buffoon. Heckled by a man of lower sensibilities, Stephen and his system are enhanced, shining the more because of these vulgarities.

Joyce, in Trieste, feeling that the artist, if he is to function as such, must function as a human being, has constructed a scene in which a talk on the eternal is interrupted by frivolous secular remarks. It is Lynch who is amused by the quoting of Aquinas. ("Are you laughing up your sleeve?") He says that a passage "has the true scholastic stink." He points out the irrelevance of "prating about beauty and the imagination in this miserable God-forsaken island." He—the court jester—is permitted to say: "I want a job of five hundred a year. You can't get me one."

Only later may we realize that we have been hearing a dialogue. It is the low-comedy relief who has the long perspective. Stephen's timeless remarks are a temporary posture. Like a stage magician, Joyce has his card before us, yet uses misdirection so that we overlook it. At the end of this scene, after these abstractions, they pass E. C. (The "silent" Stephen has told all his friends that she is the one he loves.) Lynch says to Stephen, "Your beloved is here." Stephen's mind is "emptied of theory and courage."

A few pages later, Stephen writes a poem. The moment is an

echo of the "magic" moments. He has spoken of "wholeness, harmony and radiance." We are given an example of his current product—a *fin de siècle* villanelle:

Tell no more of enchanted days.

At the end of the book, he is ready for Paris. Ulysses, Odysseus, Dedalus—he is ready to take flight. The epigraph, a phrase from Ovid, is appropriately taken from the story of Stephen's namesake. Since *A Portrait* deals with the changes in Stephen, the source, *Metamorphoses,* is equally appropriate. The phrase —"applying his mind to unknown arts"—though not a description of the early Stephen, shows the phase of development to which he is tending. In the last line, Joyce picks up the reference. "Old father, old artificer, stand me now and ever in good stead."

It is Icarus who speaks. According to the legend, he is going to fall. This is related to Stephen's moment on the beach. "To fall, to triumph, to recreate life out of life."

It has been said that, in this ending, there is confusion between father and son. That is intended. It is in falling that the son will turn into the father. The noncreative Icarus will become the Artificer. This book is *A Portrait of Dedalus as Icarus.*

Joyce was fond of saying that the Church began with a pun. *A Portrait* has a pun as its last word. "Old father, old artificer, stand me now and ever in good *stead.*" This means that Icarus asks the artificer to help him. But it also means, "Father, take my place." It is Stephen's prayer that he may be an artist. "Save me—by becoming me!"

All this lies in the future. Stephen will return to Dublin. He will go into *Ulysses,* where at the end there will be an intimation of still another metamorphosis. It is Joyce who is ready. He is announcing that he is not Stephen. He has finished *A Portrait.* He is ready to begin *Ulysses.*

[46]

SELECTED BIBLIOGRAPHY

Early Work of James Joyce

The Critical Writings of James Joyce. Ed. by Ellsworth Mason and Richard Ellmann. New York, Viking Press, 1959.

Chamber Music. Ed. by William York Tindall. New York, Columbia University Press, 1954.

Epiphanies. Introduction and notes by O. A. Silverman. Buffalo, University of Buffalo, 1956.

Stephen Hero. Ed. by Theodore Spencer. Norfolk, Conn., New Directions, 1963.

Dubliners. Corrected text. New York, Viking Press, 1967. Reprinted in Viking Critical Library, 1969.

A Portrait of the Artist as a Young Man. Corrected text. New York, Viking Press, 1964. Reprinted in Viking Critical Library, 1968.

—— With notes by J. S. Atherton. London, Heinemann, 1964.

Biographical Material

Byrne, John Francis. Silent Years. New York, Farrar, Strauss and Young, 1953.

Colum, Mary, and Padraic Colum. Our Friend James Joyce. New York, Doubleday, 1958.

Ellmann, Richard. James Joyce. New York, Oxford University Press, 1958.

Gorman, Herbert. James Joyce. New York, Rinehart, 1948.

Joyce, Stanislaus. The Dublin Diary of Stanislaus Joyce. Ithaca, Cornell University Press, 1962.

—— My Brother's Keeper. New York, Viking Press, and London, Faber and Faber, 1958.

Letters of James Joyce. Volume I, ed. by Stuart Gilbert. Volume II, ed. by Richard Ellmann. New York, Viking Press, and London, Faber and Faber, 1966.

Sullivan, Kevin. Joyce Among the Jesuits. New York, Columbia University Press, 1958.

Critical Works and Commentary

Anderson, Chester G., ed. A Portrait of the Artist as a Young Man. Viking Critical Library. New York, Viking Press, 1968.

Connolly, Thomas E., ed. Joyce's Portrait: Criticism and Critiques. New York, Appleton-Century-Crofts, 1962.

[47]

Ellmann, Richard. "The Background of the Dead," from his James Joyce. Reprinted in Scholes and Litz *(q.v.)*.

—"The Growth of Imagination," from his James Joyce. Reprinted in Anderson *(q.v.)*.

Feshbach, Sidney. "A Slow and Dark Birth," *James Joyce Quarterly,* Vol. IV, No. 4 (Summer, 1968).

Givens, Seon, ed. James Joyce: Two Decades of Criticism. New York, Vanguard Press, 1962.

Hart, Clive, ed. James Joyce's Dubliners. New York, Viking Press, and London, Faber and Faber, 1969.

Joyce, Stanislaus. "The Background to Dubliners," *The Listener,* Vol. LI (March 25, 1954).

Kelleher, John V. "Irish History and Mythology in James Joyce's 'The Dead,'" *Review of Politics,* Vol. XXVII, No. 3 (July, 1965).

Kenner, Hugh. "The Portrait in Perspective." Printed in Givens *(q.v.)*. Reprinted in Connolly and Anderson *(qq.v.)*.

Levin, Harry. James Joyce: A Critical Introduction. Norfolk, Conn., New Directions, 1941.

Magalaner, Marvin. Time of Apprenticeship. London, New York, Toronto, Abelard-Schuman, 1959

Magalaner, Marvin, and Richard M. Kain. Joyce, the Man, the Work, the Reputation. New York, New York University Press, 1956.

Scholes, Robert, and Richard M. Kain. The Workshop of Dedalus. Evanston, Ill., Northwestern University Press, 1965.

Scholes, Robert, and A. Walton Litz, eds. Dubliners. Viking Critical Library. New York, Viking Press, 1969.

Staley, Thomas F., ed. James Joyce Today. Bloomington and London, Indiana University Press, 1966.

Tindall, William York. A Reader's Guide to James Joyce. New York, Noonday Press, 1959.